Celebrating your year

1974

a very special year for

_____

_____

_____

_____

_____

A message from the author:

Welcome to the year 1974.

I trust you will enjoy this fascinating romp down memory lane.

And when you have reached the end of the book, please join me in the battle against AI generated copy-cat books and fake reviews.

Details are at the back of the book.

Best regards,
Bernard Bradforsand-Tyler.

WATERGATE SCANDAL
NIXON RESIGNS

ECONOMIC
STAGFLATION
CRISIS

CHINA'S
TERRACOTTA ARMY
DISCOVERY

Flashback to **1974** a very special year

BOMBS EXPLODE
IN LONDON

3-DAY WORK
WEEK FOR UK.

CARNATION REVOLUTION
IN PORTUGAL

ALI's Rumble in the Jungle

Contents

Let's flashback to 1974, a very special year.

Was this the year you were born?

Was this the year you were married?

Whatever the reason, this book is a celebration of your year,

THE YEAR 1974.

Turn the pages to discover a book packed with fun-filled
fabulous facts. We look at the people, the places, the
politics and the pop culture that made 1974 unique
and helped shape the world we know today.

So get your time-travel suit on, and enjoy this trip down memory
lane, to rediscover what life was like, back in the year 1974.

Imagine if time-travel was a reality, and one fine morning you wake up to find yourself flashed back in time, back to the year 1974.

What would life be like for a typical family, in a typical town, somewhere in America?

1974 was a troubled year for Americans. The year began with a crisis in the global economy caused by the ongoing Arab oil embargo. Sky-high crude oil prices, rising and persistently high inflation, high unemployment and a stagnant economy combined in a rare economic combination known as stagflation.

Protesters outside the White House calling for President Nixon's impeachment, 1974.

To add to the misery, we were faced with a crisis of government—a political scandal so immense it would bring down a president and shake our faith in our political institutions.

By the end of the year, we were coping with a four-fold increase in oil prices, crippling inflation, soaring unemployment, a crash on Wall Street, and the worst recession since the 1930s.

In the ten years to 1974, the US population had increased by 10% to 209.3 million.[1] Americans accounted for only 5.3% of the world's population, yet consumed a whopping 33% of the world's energy. The US economy accounted for a quarter of global production.

The Baby Boomers had become a large, vocal population of young adults. Birth rates and family sizes continued to fall, thanks to changing family values and readily available contraceptives.

Universities and colleges became breeding grounds for free-thinking, liberal theories. Students often shared accommodation, partly for cost savings, but also as an expression of a new way of living, cohabiting, exploring sexual freedoms and spiritual fulfillment.

Rock concert audience at Palm Beach International Raceway, 4th August 1974.

The hippie view of the world, with its emphasis on peace, love and nature, had focused our collective attention on the anti-war, anti-pollution, and anti-consumerism movements. The Watergate scandal and the rising cost of living and unemployment levels reinforced our rejection of our parents' old traditions and conservative values. Our distrust and disgust for authority and for the status quo increased further. Environmentalists, African Americans, LGBT and other minority communities ramped up the fight for recognition and equality.

[1] worldometers.info/world-population/us-population/.

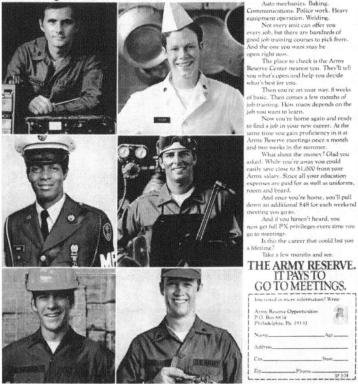
Learn a Skill That Could Last You a Lifetime. In Just a Few Months.

Auto mechanics. Baking. Communications. Police work. Heavy equipment operation. Welding.

Not every unit can offer you every job, but there are hundreds of good job training courses to pick from. And the one you want may be open right now.

The place to check is the Army Reserve Center nearest you. They'll tell you what's open and help you decide what's best for you.

Then you're on your way. 8 weeks of basic. Then comes a few months of job training. How many depends on the job you want to learn.

Now you're home again and ready to find a job in your new career. At the same time you gain proficiency in it at Army Reserve meetings once a month and two weeks in the summer.

What about the money? Glad you asked. While you're away you could easily save close to $1,000 from your Army salary. Since all your education expenses are paid for as well as uniforms, room and board.

And once you're home, you'll pull down an additional $48 for each weekend meeting you go to.

And if you haven't heard, you now get full PX privileges every time you go to meetings.

Is this the career that could last you a lifetime?

Take a few months and see.

The Army Reserve. It Pays To Go To Meetings.

At the same time, the feminist movement had been gaining momentum. Women were achieving higher levels of education in greater numbers, increasing in confidence and independence. Divorce rates were rising steeply. An estimated 50% of couples who married in 1974 would end up divorced in future years.[1]

Two landmark acts were passed in 1974. The *Women's Educational Equity Act* provided protections against gender discrimination in education, and the *Equal Credit Opportunity Act* banned discrimination against credit applicants on the basis of sex, marital status, age, religion or race. Before this, unmarried women could not access credit, and married women required their husbands to co-sign their credit applications.

Women were also added to the list of protected classes in *The Housing and Community Development Act* of 1974. This ensured home owners could no longer refuse to sell or rent to a woman, charge extra fees, add extra rules, or sexually harass a woman tenant or buyer.

Women attendees at the National Organization for Women (NOW) conference in Houston, May '74.

Average costs in 1974 [4]	
New house	$29,966
New car	$4,095
Dishwasher	$168
Vacuum cleaner	$69
A gallon of gasoline	$0.39

In 1974 the median family income was $12,840 per year.[2] Unemployment stood at 7.2%, with negative GDP growth at -05%.[3]

[1] nationalaffairs.com/publications/detail/the-evolution-of-divorce.
[2] census.gov/programs-surveys/ahs/data/1974/ahs-1974-summary-tables0/ahs-national-report.html.
[3] thebalance.com/unemployment-rate-by-year-3305506.
[4] thepeoplehistory.com and mclib.info/reference/local-history-genealogy/historic-prices/.

For Christmas, Smith-Corona presents the typewriter of The Cartridge Age.

With the cartridge you can change to a fresh ribbon in just 3 seconds.

With the cartridge you can change to a correction ribbon in just 3 seconds.

With the cartridge you can change to a color ribbon in just 3 seconds.

If you're looking for a very special Christmas gift, we'd like to suggest a very special typewriter. The Smith-Corona Cartridge Ribbon Typewriter. It's the only electric portable with a snap-out, snap-in cartridge ribbon system.

In 3 seconds you can snap out a worn ribbon and snap in a fresh ribbon.

In 3 seconds you can snap out a black ribbon and snap in any of five color ribbons.

In 3 seconds you can snap in a carbon film ribbon that makes typing look like professional printing.

In 3 seconds you can snap in a correction ribbon that allows you to correct errors more neatly and with less effort than ever before.

The Smith-Corona Cartridge Ribbon Typewriter for Christmas. It's the most advanced electric portable typewriter you can give.

Picture yourself, Pronto!

The new Pronto! has a self-timer that puts you in your own picture!

With this new self-timer Pronto!, the fun is automatic. And so's the camera! Just set the distance and timer, then join the fun in front of the camera. Now get ready! The camera will set the exposure and go off automatically. In minutes, you'll have a sharp, clear SX-70 picture—and you're in it!

You'll have all the laughter of that moment for many years to come, too. Because the brilliant colors of SX-70 pictures last.

SX-70 pictures are more fun than ever with a new self-timer Pronto! Because after all, you ought to be in pictures.

Polaroid's New Pronto!

The new Pronto! Has a self-timer that puts you in your own picture!

With this new self-timer Pronto! the fun is automatic. And so's the camera! Just set the distance and timer, then join the fun in front of the camera. Now get ready! The camera will set the exposure and go off automatically. In minutes, you'll have a sharp, clear SX-70 picture—and you're in it!

You'll have all the laughter of that moment for many years to come, too. Because the brilliant colors of SX-70 pictures last.

SX-70 pictures are more fun than ever with a new self-timer Pronto! Because after all, you ought to be in pictures.

Now just imagine you flashed back to a town in 1974 in the United Kingdom. Just as for their American counterparts, the impact of the Arab oil embargo hit hard.

The joyful, carefree optimism of England's *Swinging Sixties* could not last forever. The sentiment on the streets had shifted from frivolity to revolution. This was echoed in the music, arts, culture, and street fashion.

The country faced its first post-war recession as inflation soared above 16%, rising even further the following year. Higher living costs resulted in wage increase demands, causing an economic crisis known as a wage-price spiral.

The decade of the '70s was marred by continuous industrial strife. Power struggles between the government and the powerful trade unions peaked in the early '70s, and would plunge the country into darkness when Prime Minister Edward Heath declared a three-day work week to save electricity. His tough stance on the unions did not win favor with the electorate. Following a snap election in March '74, resulting a hung parliament, Heath would resign as Prime Minister after failing to form a coalition government.

To add to the uncertainties that plagued 1974, the incoming government of Harold Wilson called a second general election to be held in October of the same year.

North Shields, Tyneside residents in 1974.

British feminists had a long-established history of activism and continued to grow in numbers and strength throughout the 1970s.

The newly formed Women's Liberation Movement quickly grew to become a national movement, with thousands of grassroots groups. Their list of equal rights demands included equal pay, equal education, and free contraception.

Women march through London for International Women's Day, March 1974.

In 1974 the average age of marriage for women was 25, and the average age for the birth of their first child was 26.[1] The fertility rate dropped to 1.9 births per woman, substantially down from the peak of 2.9 in 1964,[2] and the first time the rate dipped below 2.0. The contraceptive pill (available since 1961) and the legalization of abortion in 1967 aided in this decline.

In the early '70s, around 50% of British families owned a car.[3] Within the larger cities, most people still relied on public transport.

The rate of car ownership had been steadily increasing in the years before 1974 (around 3% growth per year). However, this growth stagnated for the five years to follow as a result of the oil crisis and economic recession.

[1&2] ons.gov.uk/peoplepopulationandcommunity.
[3] ons.gov.uk/ons/rel/ghs/general-lifestyle-survey/2011/rpt-40-years.html.

Beautiful. And that's only the beginning.

Chances are, there's a handsome Kodak Carousel custom H projector that has all the features you could want just as it is. Whether it's automatic focus, automatic timing, or remote control.

It's also nice to know that other options are available to increase its versatility. Everything from special purpose lenses, a stack loader, slide clips, to special "presentation aids" that let you synchronize a taped narrative and music with your slides.

So go to your photo dealer, discuss your needs, and see the Kodak Carousel custom H projector in action. The 860H shown is less than $255. Other Kodak Carousel projectors from less than $75.

Prices are subject to change without notice.

Kodak Carousel custom H projectors.

Beautiful. And that's only the beginning.

Chances are, there's a handsome Kodak Carousel custom H projector that has all the features you could want just as it is. Whether it's automatic focus, automatic timing, or remote control.

It's also nice to know that other options are available to increase its versatility. Everything from special purpose lenses, a stack loader, slide clips, to special "presentation aids" that let you synchronize a taped narrative and music with your slides.

So go to your photo dealer, discuss your needs, and see the Kodak Carousel custom H projector in action. The 860H shown is less than $255. Other Kodak Carousel projectors from less than $75.

Kodak Carousel custom H projectors.

By 1974, the UK was nearly half-way through repaying its post-war debt to America and Canada. The 20-year post-war building boom, which had kept cash flowing and unemployment low, was over.

Economic growth in the UK was only half that of Germany and Japan, with annual GDP having slipped from 2nd place in 1960 (behind only USA), to 6th place in 1974. Moreover, UK GDP per capita had fallen to 29th place in world rankings.[1]

By 1974, most of the former colonies of the United Kingdom had been granted independence. The cost to keep, maintain and defend them had proven too heavy a burden.

The "Troubles" in Northern Ireland had been raging for decades. Irish Nationalist campaigns became increasingly daring, spilling into streets across the UK as activists took to bombing targets in major cities, including central London.

London teachers on the march for a London allowance, 29th April 1974.

Nurses strike for better pay at the Shropshire Orthopaedic Hospital, Oswestry , 3rd May 1974.

Across the nation, marches, protests, riots, industrial strife and strikes were increasing. The UK in 1974 was a country in turmoil. And this was just the beginning. The worse was yet to come.

The remainder of the decade would bring a mounting series of economic crises, industrial actions and major political battles.

[1] nationmaster.com/country-info/stats/Economy/GDP.

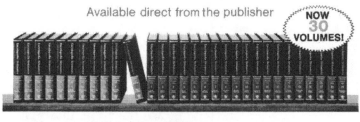

Instead of a hamburger...
make Armour Vienna Sausage the meat in your meals.

You'll love the out-of-the-ordinary taste that Armour Vienna Sausage adds to your meals.

Each sausage has been cooked in a hearty beef broth. And they're all plump with beef and pork—so plump, you can hardly get them out of the can!

Try using Armour Vienna Sausage in all kinds of dishes—like this Five Star Casserole. You'll find it makes a tasty change to the hamburger meat routine.

By the early '70s, the Baby Boomers were young adults. Everything about them was a break-away from their parents: their music, their fashion, their values, their personal and sexual freedoms. They were non-traditional, non-conformist, anti-authority, anti-consumerist, anti-war, politically active, experimental drug users, hippies, believers and disbelievers. Anything was possible. Everything was acceptable.

The rise of communal living and "Back to the Land" movement of the late '60s and early '70s were lifestyle expressions of freedom of choice. Communes were anti-establishment and experimental, communes were whatever the inhabitants chose them to be. Up to 3000 communes existed in the USA during this period.[1]

In Vermont, a haven for hippies, an estimated one third of young adults (below age 34) were living communally.[2]

[1&2] forbes.com/sites/russellflannery/
2021/04/11/what-happened-to-
Americas-communes/?sh=7454bc05c577.

Most communes encouraged co-ownership of possessions, collective chores and shared child-raising. For many, clothes, monogamy and drug usage were optional. By rejecting the 40-hour work week, many communards relied on food stamps, or temporary odd jobs to keep themselves nourished.

In rural areas communards practiced living off the land, setting up farms, building their own houses, creating and selling handicrafts.

Myrtle Hill Farm, Vermont.

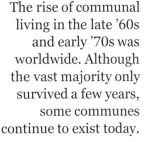

A geodesic dome house in Myrtle Hill Farm, Vermont. Recalls one communard, "In 1971 a young man named Bernie Sanders visited Myrtle Hill Farm... Sanders' tendency to just sit around talking politics and avoid actual physical labor got him the boot."[1]

Communards at Hog Farm, California.

The rise of communal living in the late '60s and early '70s was worldwide. Although the vast majority only survived a few years, some communes continue to exist today.

[1] From *We Are As Gods: Back to the Land in the 1970s on the Quest for a New America* by Brian Doherty.

1974 Thunderbird Burgundy Special Edition.

Most of the luxuries in Thunderbird come *standard:* things like air conditioning. The vinyl roof. Steel-belted radial ply tires. And it doesn't require premium gas. Now, for a little more, you can have this very limited Special Edition. The Burgundy Luxury Group is sumptuous, from its discreet gold stripes and distinctive wire wheel covers, to its deep Victoria Velour seating surfaces (or choose red leather and vinyl). Here's the car to remember. Better still, to own. Thunderbird 1974. *In the world of personal luxury cars, it's the unique value.*

This is your year. Make a little Thunder of your own.

Automotive Industry in Decline

By the time the Arab oil embargo was lifted in March 1974, oil prices had soared four-fold, and gas prices at the pump had increased 40% from the pre-embargo prices. Unfortunately, the end of the embargo did not bring with it any reduction in oil prices. The impact on the automotive industry was sustained and severe.

Sales of new cars declined as the recession deepened and consumer confidence plummeted. Assembly plants were among the many businesses to layoff workers.

Traffic congestion in New York City, 1974.

By June '74, about 10% of US gas stations had closed due to lack of supply and financial loss, with 6% of auto-related retail establishments forced out of business.[1]

Waiting in line for gas during the oil embargo.

[1] From the New York Times, 1974/09/25 archives.

Throughout the '70's, Detroit remained the car manufacturing center of America, where "the Big Three" (Ford, General Motors and Chrysler) produced the bulk of cars sold. Although still renowned for their gas-guzzling "muscle cars", consumers responded to the oil crisis by shifting to more compact, fuel-efficient cars. US manufacturers were under growing pressure from the increasingly popular, more affordable and cheaper-to-run imports.

American muscle cars battled to maintain relevance and dominance. These high-performance coupes with large, powerful V-8 engines and rear-wheel drive had been designed to satisfy our desire for power above all else. But the introduction of the *Clean Air Act* of 1970 forced automakers to drastically reduce emission pollutants. Clean air equipment became the new focus, robbing engines of much of their raw power and performance.

The new Ford Mustang II.
It just may be the best news from Detroit
in 9½ years.

Plymouth Gold Duster by Chrysler, 1974.

Mercury Comet GT 2-Door Sedan by Ford, 1974.

American auto makers responded to the stricter federal requirements, and to the increased competition from imports, by creating their own compact and sub-compact fuel-efficient car models. However poor design, inadequate engineering and manufacturing led to a stream of disasters, damaging the customer experience.

Five car-producing countries dominated the industry in 1974: Japan, Germany, England, and France, with America in the top spot. Japan's meteoric rise into this elite group had been particularly aggressive, and their cars stood poised to dominate the world markets.

Japanese cars were reliable, affordable, compact, efficient and popular, quickly making Toyota, Nissan, Mitsubishi, Mazda, Datsun, and Honda the export market leaders. Japanese car exports increased nearly 200-fold in the ten years to 1974.

As we became more aware of the hidden dangers and impracticalities inherent in American car designs, European and Japanese cars were seen as more reliable, safer and more fuel efficient.

In the early '70s, the Volkswagen Beetle became the world's best-selling car. However, competition from Japanese cars saw Beetle sales plummet by 12% in 1974. Volkswagen was in financial crisis, announcing its first ever yearly loss. The automaker responded with a new generation of water-cooled, front-wheel drive cars—the Golf.

1974 MERCURY COUGAR XR-7

In size, this new breed of Cougar is like Grand Prix and Monte Carlo.
In every other way, it's like nobody else's car.

You're looking at the all new Cougar for '74. It's more than a new car. It's moved up one whole class. In fact Cougar is the only new choice among the mid-size personal luxury cars.

There's new styling, inside and out. New dash with tachometer and hooded gauges mounted in deeply padded vinyl. Elegant new opera window. Distinctive new Landau roof. Steel-belted radials. All standard. There's power steering. And front disc brakes, automatic floor shift and bucket seats, also standard. Plus the same type suspension system as Lincoln-Mercury's most expensive luxury car. Other features shown are optional.

And along with Cougar's new size class comes a whole new class of comfort for you. Because we felt this much luxury deserved a little more room.

MERCURY COUGAR

LINCOLN-MERCURY DIVISION

In size, this new breed of Cougar is like Grand Prix and Monte Carlo.
In every other way, its like nobody else's car.

You're looking at the all new Cougar for '74. It's more than a new car. It's moved up one whole class. In fact Cougar is the only new choice among the mid-size personal luxury cars.

There's new styling, inside and out. New dash with tachometer and hooded gauges mounted in deeply padded vinyl. Elegant new opera window. Distinctive new Landau roof. Steel-belted radials. All standard. There's power steering. And front disc brakes, automatic floor shift and bucket seats, also standard. Plus the same type suspension system as Lincoln-Mercury's most expensive luxury car. Other features shown are optional.

And along with Cougar's new size class comes a whole new class of comfort for you. Because we felt this much luxury deserved a little more room.

GM gets very personal when it comes to cars.

There are some 210 million people in the United States, no two alike.

They express themselves in the way they dress, the things they do and the cars they drive—which is one reason why General Motors builds so many kinds of personal cars.

We build America's only production two-seat sports car. America's only cars with front-wheel drive. And America's only convertibles.

We build luxurious personal cars, sporty personal cars and personal cars that are both sporty and luxurious.

The way we see it, if you want a car that says something about you, we want to help you say it.

GM. We want you to drive what you like and like what you drive.

The political crisis known as "Watergate" spanned two years, beginning in mid-1972 and culminating with the downfall of the president in August 1974. The scandal shook and shocked the nation, damaging our faith and trust in government. Named after the Watergate building in Washington D.C., the term has become synonymous with conspiracy and political corruption at the highest levels, so much so that the suffix –*gate*, can now be attached to any name to suggest extreme scandal or controversy.

In mid-1972, members of President Nixon's re-election committee broke into the Democratic National Committee's headquarters in the Watergate building. They stole documents and bugged the phones.

Movies about Watergate, *All the President's Men* (Warner Bros. 1976) and *The Post* (20th Century Fox, 2017).

On their return visit, they were caught by a vigilant guard. The President vehemently denied having links to the "burglars", while secretly paying hush money to cover-up the crimes, and instructing the CIA to obstruct an FBI investigation. The public believed his lies, giving him a landslide re-election victory.

Frustrated by the web of lies, an FBI whistle-blower known as Deep Throat provided *Washington Post* reporters Bob Woodward and Carl Bernstein with damning proof of clandestine and illegal espionage activities orchestrated from within the White House.

The trials for the burglars exposed direct connections to the President, leading the Senate to appoint an investigative committee to hold further hearings.

Watergate newspaper headlines from 1973 and 1974.

Nixon Knew of I am not a crook, Cover-Up Plan Nixon declares

FORD GIVES PARDON TO NIXON, WHO REGRETS 'MY MISTAKES'

NIXON WON'T, 3 Top Nixon Aides

RELEASE TAPES Tied to Cover-Up

President Taped Talks, Phone Calls;

On 17th May 1973, live daily broadcasts of the Watergate hearings began, lasting seven months. 85% of US households tuned in to radio or simultaneous broadcasts on CBS, NBC and ABC. Outraged viewers watched as the Senate Select Committee on Presidential Campaign Activities uncovered widespread evidence of political espionage, bribery, kidnapping, evidence tampering, and illegal wire-tapping of thousands of citizens.

When the Committee subpoenaed the recorded voice tapes of the Oval Office, President Nixon refused, citing executive privilege. The Committee voted to impeach the President for obstruction of justice, abuse of power, and contempt of Congress. This stand-off went all the way to the Supreme Court, where claims of executive privilege were voided. Nixon was ordered to release the tapes. On 30th July 1974, President Nixon complied.

The Oval Office tapes confirmed that Nixon had lied to the Nation for more than two years. He had been actively involved in illegal crimes and cover-ups from the beginning.

With certain conviction awaiting, Nixon resigned on 9th August 1974. He remains the only US president to have resigned from office. He was succeeded by Gerald Ford, his Vice President. On 8th September 1974, President Ford granted Nixon a full and unconditional pardon.

In all, 69 people were indicted and 48 were convicted as a result of Watergate—many of them top Nixon officials.

Demonstrators in Washington DC. 22nd Oct 1973.

President Nixon, Pat Nixon, Vice President Ford, and Betty Ford walking from the White House to the President's Helicopter, 9th Aug 1974.

President Ford announcing his decision to grant a full pardon to President Nixon, 8th Sept 1974.

Yom Kippur War

Egyptian forces crossing the Suez Canal into the Sinai Peninsula.

On 6th October 1973, the Jewish holiday of Yom Kippur, a coalition of Arab states led by Egypt and Syria launched a surprise attack against Israel. Egyptian troops swept into Sinai Peninsula, while Syrian troops invaded the Golan Heights. Both nations aimed to take back regions they had lost to Israel during the six-day war of 1967.

With the Soviets supporting the Arab coalition, the US felt compelled to aid Israel by sending a full-scale air-lift of military equipment. The region had become a Cold War battleground.

Most of the heavy fighting ceased within a few weeks following a UN brokered ceasefire. However clashes continued along front-lines well into 1974. The possibility of renewed full-scale war, with the involvement of nuclear-ready superpowers, was ever-present.

The build-up of vessels in the Mediterranean Sea was the largest ever seen during the Cold War. By May 1974, the US had 60 naval vessels stationed there, including 9 submarines and 3 aircraft carriers. The Soviets had 97 vessels ready for battle, including 23 submarines.

Political tensions and military conflicts between Israel and various Arab states continue to this day.

Israeli troops retake the Sinai Peninsula, Oct 1973.

OPEC Oil Embargo and Oil Crisis

In response to US support for Israel during the Yom Kippur War, the Arab members of the Organization of Petroleum Exporting Countries (OPEC) imposed an oil embargo directly targeting the US and other allies of Israel. Oil shipments to the USA, the UK, Canada, Japan, and other nations were immediately suspended. These countries all relied on oil supplies from the Middle East, causing immediate shortages. Although the embargo was lifted in March 1974, the shortage of oil lasted well into 1975.

The lack of alternative providers caused an immediate jump in the price of oil. Prices continued rising, from $2.90 a barrel before the embargo, to nearly $12 a barrel by March 1974. Oil prices remained high even after the embargo was lifted. The impact of this increase on the global economy was significant and severe.

In response to the embargo, the US government imposed fuel rationing and lowered speed limits to reduce consumption.

Gas stations ran out of fuel as motorists queued to fill up. Prices could rise several times a day, causing motorists to panic-buy.

In the US, businesses strained under soaring oil prices and a falling dollar, with many closing or laying off workers. Unemployment rose sharply, GDP plummeted to negative figures (-0.50% in 1974) and lack of liquidity triggered a massive stock market crash.

A similar scenario played out across much of the world, and the period 1973-'75 would be plagued by economic recession. The oil crisis had highlighted the importance of energy security and the need for alternative energy sources and conservation measures.

Moto-Bike: For tough kids.

The boy. Designed to run, jump, take spills, and somehow come out in the same shape he started.

The Moto-Bike. He can expect it to go just about anywhere he wants to take it, and still come back in one piece. (It was designed for the demanding new sport of bicycle motocross.)

Wide motocross handlebars for better control.

Rugged tires. So he can get out of the mud as fast as he gets in it.

Swing arm rear suspensions makes the bumps a lot easier on the bike. And on the boy.

Oil damped front forks. They take the shocks, instead of the rider.

Plus motorcycle grips, heavy duty frame, and a lot of other racing details you'll find on no other bike. See the Moto-Bike now only at your Yamaha Dealer.

The Moto-Bike, from Yamaha.

Desegregation Busing

In 1954, the landmark *Brown vs. Board of Education* Supreme Court decision upheld that racial segregation of children in public schools was unconstitutional. States were ordered to integrate their schools.

Twenty years later, school integration had failed to improve. Well-funded schools with highly educated teachers in white neighborhoods generally produced successful white graduates, while dilapidated, overpopulated, understaffed and underfunded schools with ill-trained teachers in socially disadvantaged black neighborhoods turned out far less educated students. De facto school segregation continued to exist as a direct result of neighborhood segregation.

On 21st June 1974, a court in Massachusetts ruled in favor of desegregation busing. White students would be bused to black schools, and black students would be bused to white schools.

Angry protests by white middle-class parents erupted.

Above: Parents protest in Boston, June 1974.

Below: White students outside Boston's Hyde Park High School, 12th Dec 1974.

On the first day only 13 white students attended school in Roxbury, while 100 (of the 1300 selected black students) showed up at South Boston High School. They faced abuse, hurled eggs, bottles and bricks. State troopers guarded the schools for years.

"White flight" saw middle-class families move to areas not affected by busing, while hundreds of thousands of public school students moved to private schools.

Desegregation busing continued in Boston for 14 years, and longer in other states. Ultimately, integration may have been achieved, but studies have shown race relations and academic standards across the board worsened as a direct result of the busing programs.

Planned un-obsolescence.

Your phone is built to last...and last. Bell System phones are designed and built to withstand "torture tests" equal to 20 years average use. Of course, you may not need your phone that long because you'll move, or want to get a newer model.

Also, the phones we collect, we recycle. Practically nothing goes to waste.

The Bell Telephone Companies know you want a dependable, reliable phone.

We hear you.

Nuclear Bomb Testing

Remember when dropping nuclear bombs was commonplace? For more than 40 years, the Nuclear Arms Race gave the USA and USSR the pretext needed to test nuclear bombs on a massive scale. Nearly 1,700 bombs were dropped by the superpowers, most of them during the '60s and '70s. A further 300 were tested by China, France, and the UK. These tests served to understand the effectiveness and capacity of each bomb type. They also acted as a deterrent to enemy nations.

In 1974, the US carried out 22 tests, mostly at the Nevada Proving Grounds, while the USSR carried out 21 tests. All were underground tests, in keeping with the 1962 *Partial Nuclear Test Ban* which prohibited atmospheric, outer-space, and underwater testing.

France continued to ignore the Test Ban, conducting nine atmospheric nuclear tests over the Pacific Islands.

On 18th May, India became the sixth nuclear power, testing an underground atomic bomb code-named *Operation Smiling Buddha*.

Although most of the test sites were largely uninhabited by humans, some of them were densely populated. The effects of radioactive fallout plagued local populations for years afterward.

Underground nuclear test at the Nevada Proving Grounds, USA, in the early '70s.

Operation Smiling Buddha detonated at the Pokhran Test Range, in Rajasthan, India, 18th May 1974.

IRA Bombs Britain

The 30-year-long nationalist campaign in Northern Ireland, known as *The Troubles*, peaked in the early '70s as Roman Catholic Republicans (IRA) fought against Protestant Ulster Unionists and the British military. Although often mistaken for a war of religion, *The Troubles* was in fact a political war. The Republicans were fighting for the reunification of Northern Ireland with the Republic of Ireland. The Unionists sought to keep Northern Ireland as part of the UK.

British troops patrolled Northern Ireland's streets for 37 years. Although their role was officially neutral, they were condemned for covertly supporting the Unionists, and were permitted to imprison IRA suspects without trial.

Part of the aftermath of a PIRA bomb at Westminster Hall. Houses of Parliament, London. 17th June 1974.

Emergency services at the site of the Birmingham pub bombings. 21st Nov 1974.

A total of 21 miles (34 km) of Peace Walls were built in Northern Ireland to physically separate Republicans from Unionist neighborhoods. In recent years these walls have become something of a tourist attraction.

By 1974, the Provisional IRA (militant faction of the IRA) expanded its Mainland Campaign, bringing their terror to the streets of Britain. They exploded bombs in major cities on British buses and in crowded pubs, clubs and bars. In central London bombs were exploded at the Tower of London, the Houses of Parliament, Victoria Station, Kings Cross, Piccadilly Circus, and on Oxford Street.

3-Day Work Week for the UK

Soaring inflation and a cap on public sector pay rises left many British workers struggling from a drop in real wages. In October 1973, the powerful National Union of Mineworkers (NUM) demanded a fair deal for its members—a 35% pay increase to bring salaries on par with other industries. The ruling Conservative Party soundly rejected the request.

NUM members voted against strike action, choosing a ban on overtime instead. The ban halved electricity supply overnight, as coal stockpiles had been largely depleted during previous miner's strikes. Electricity supply struggled to keep up with the winter demand.

In a bid to lower usage, Prime Minister Edward Heath announced a three-day work week to commence 1st Jan 1974. Electricity would be rationed to homes on a rotational basis. Millions were laid-off as business struggled to remain operational.

Employees working by candlelight, Jan 1974.

Five weeks later, NUM members voted in favor of a full strike, having rejected the National Coal Board's 16% pay rise offer.

Assuming public support for tough government over trade union demands, Heath called a snap general election. He did not win re-election.

The miner's strike and the three-day work week lasted until Mar '74. Its end was brought about by the return of Harold Wilson (prime minister 1964-'70 and 1974-'76), and his agreement to the full 35% wage increase.

A 3-DAY WEEK BRITAIN

MILLIONS of workers will go on to a three or four-day week from Monday unless the miners' leaders decide today to order a ballot on the Coal Board's pay offer.

Rotas are being drawn up by the Electricity Boards and firms will be forbidden to use electricity for two days a week.

Keeping up your spirits!
BY HARVEY ELLIOTT
BRITONS are deter-

On 25th April 1974, a military coup staged by officers of Portugal's Armed Forces overthrew the 40-year-long fascist dictatorship of the Estado Novo Regime. The right-wing, anti-democratic regime, installed in 1933, was known to torture, imprison or execute its opponents. It was opposed to communism, socialism, and liberalism. While the rest of the world's colonies had gained (or were demanding) independence from their colonial powers, Portugal's nationalist regime had been determined to hold on to its colonies.

The secret signal for the officers to begin their coup was the playing of two selected songs on the radio. Within six hours, the coup had succeeded. Citizens flooded the streets to celebrate, turning the coup into a popular revolution. Gathering around Lisbon's flower market, some of the military insurgents put carnations in their gun barrels. The images were broadcast on televisions worldwide.

Portuguese soldiers relax with carnations in their gun barrels, 25th April 1974.

A crowd celebrates on an armored vehicle in Lisbon, 25th April 1974.

For the remainder of 1974 and all of 1975, power struggles were waged between differing political groups. Portugal held its first free election on 25th April 1975, becoming a democratic country on 25th April 1976 with the enactment of its new constitution.

In 1974, Portugal had the lowest literacy rate and lowest GDP per capita in Western Europe. It trailed its European neighbors in the fields of healthcare, education, infrastructure and agriculture. It has since emerged as a peaceful, stable and developed democratic nation.

Independence for Portugal's Colonies

The cost for Portugal to maintain control over its African colonies had exacted a heavy financial toll on its economy. Up to 40% of the country's budget was being spent annually fighting the "War of Liberation" in Angola, Guinea-Bissau and Mozambique. Following the Carnation Revolution, Portugal's new government promptly ended the unpopular and expensive war.

Portuguese returnees from Angola, 1975.

Half a million "returnees", mostly white Portuguese settlers, arrived in Lisbon during 1974-'75. They were offered assistance with food, finance and accommodation. However, many returning families had lived in Africa for generations, and many had never set foot in Portugal before. Far from returning home, they felt like refugees. They had been forcibly removed from their comfortable and prosperous lives as the colonizer, settler minority.

Portugal granted full independence to Guinea-Bissau in Sept 1974. The impoverished West African state has been subject to multiple coups since, and remains one of the world's most fragile nations.

Mozambique achieved its independence on 8th Sept 1975. The sudden exodus of Portuguese professionals and tradesmen left the country without the expertise to maintain its infrastructure and economic systems. Cuba and the Soviet Union sent advisors, however Mozambique remains one of the poorest and least developed countries in the world.

Cuban and Angolan soldiers during weapons practice.

Angola was granted independence on 11th Nov 1975, ending its 13-year-long guerilla war with Portugal and marking the start of a violent civil war which would last 27 years. Three main parties battled for power. With one party gaining US support and another winning Soviet assistance, Angola quickly became a Cold War battleground.

Let yourself go. The new CB-360G.

Move out of present time. And present space. Onto a new road. A promising new place. Let good things happen to you.

Do it all. With very little gas. On the all-new Honda CB-360G. Perhaps the finest expression of the mid-size road bike concept ever built.

Engineers have a word that describes great machines. It's elegant. And the new CB-360G is the word.

Honda designers really turned on the ideas. This new 356cc twin overhead cam engine delivers a new store of low- and mid-range power. Power that flows smooth, sure, through a new six-speed transmission. (Yes, *six*-speed!)

You'll like the dependable hydraulic disc brake up front. The positive return throttle system. And the plushy creature comforts, too. A deep-cushioned seat. Rakish handlebars. Big mirrors. Redesigned instruments.

The 360 look. An altogether new form. A frame long, low, lithe. Accentuated by a shapely fuel tank. Clean new front forks. Sensational new pipes.

The CB-360G. Beautiful! Enjoy it now at your nearby Honda dealer's.

Honda. Good things happen on a Honda.

The Endangered Species Act

Since 1st January 1974, thousands of animals, plants and ecosystems have been listed under the *Endangered Species Act* (ESA) as under threat of extinction. The act, signed into law by President Nixon a few days earlier, was seen as a huge win for the conservation movement at a time when ecological issues were not given much consideration. Under the ESA, US federal agencies would be required to implement plans to aid in the conservation and recovery of any species listed as threatened or endangered, including their habitats.

Human encroachment, flora and fauna habitat destruction, pollution, hunting, and collecting, had caused an exponential rise in threatened species and extinctions throughout the 20th Century.

The year 1974 also prepared for a parallel worldwide ecological act—the *Convention on International Trade in Endangered Species of Wild Fauna and Flora* (CITES). The act sought to protect endangered species from the threats of international trade, mostly for luxury, medical or collector desires. Countries were given until 31st Dec '74 to sign the convention, which came into force in July '75. There are now 184 member countries.

The peregrine falcon and the gray wolf are some of the animals saved due to actions under the ESA.

Nixon signing into law the Endangered Species Act, 28th Dec 1973.

Terracotta Army Discovered

On 29th March 1974, local farmers pulled up a pottery sculpted head while digging a well in Xi'an, China. Additional fragments formed a life-size clay soldier, complete with armor and weapons. Government archaeologists soon found thousands of similar soldiers, each one with unique facial features and bronze accessories.

Interred for more than 2,000 years, the find is considered one of the greatest archaeological discoveries of modern times. An entire army of life-size soldiers, horses and chariots has been discovered arranged in military formation over a vast area. It is believed to be part of an elaborate mausoleum created to accompany Emperor Qin, the first emperor of China, to his afterlife.

The army comprises an estimated 8,000 soldiers, of which around 2,000 have been uncovered to date. As very few are found intact, the pain-staking restoration process has been a major challenge for archaeologists.

Magnavox announces the most significant TV breakthrough since color. The STAR™ System.

What a difference watching a Magnavox.

A new way to watch TV...by computer. The Magnavox STAR System is a limited-edition color TV console that combines the convenience of remote control with the automation of a computer. STAR lets you tune to all 82 VHF and UHF channels...instantly, directly, silently. Without any fine-tuning. And...without any searching.

To tune into Channel 15, for example, just press Digits 1 and 5 on the hand-held computer transmitter, and you're there. Electronically.

A large 15 lights up on the TV screen for three seconds to prove it. The number then disappears so you can view the program without distraction. If you forget which channel you're tuned to, a Recall button reminds you by making the number reappear.

Other transmitter buttons–On/Off, Volume Up, Down and Mute–combine to give you complete control over your Magnavox color TV. And what a color TV it is!

Magnavox Videomatic. The exclusive color TV in every STAR. No other color TV offers so many advancements in design, workmanship and reliability: • Super bright 25" (diagonal) black matrix picture tube for exceptionally bright, sharp pictures. • Automatically adjusts its own pictures to changing roomlight–for a great picture in any light. • One-button turning. The most completely automatic you can get in any TV. • 100% solid-state–no chassis tubes to burn out. Plus voltage regulators to protect critical components against powerline surges and "brownout." • Extra tested 24 straight hours for extra reliability. Of the five leading makers of solid state color TV's, only Magnavox checks each set this thoroughly. • It's no wonder so many Magnavox solid-state color TV models have been top-rated by leading consumer testing magazines in their latest reviews. See the STAR at your Magnavox dealer.

Tuning in to Television

The television was our must-have appliance of the mid-20th century, taking pride of place in our family or living rooms. By 1974, nearly every US household owned a television, with 67% of them being color sets. Although color TVs had been around since the early '50s, and color broadcasts had become commonplace since the mid-'60s, the switch from black and white to color in homes had been very slow.

Outside the USA, countries like Canada and the UK were catching up with color TV ownership and broadcasting. Australia, however, would wait till 1975 for its first color television broadcasts.

Elsewhere in the world, rates of television ownership lagged even further behind.

In many countries, television networks were government owned or subsidized, allowing for more focus on serious documentaries and news, without the constant concern of generating advertising revenue.

Carroll O'Connor and Mike Evans in *All in the Family* (CBS. 1971-1979).

Most Popular TV Shows of 1974

1	All in the Family	11	The Mary Tyler Moore Show
2	Sanford and Son	12	The Rockford Files
3	Chico and the Man	13	Little House on the Prairie
4	The Jeffersons	14	Kojak
5	M*A*S*H	15	Police Woman
6	Rhoda	16	S.W.A.T.
7	Good Times	17	The Bob Newhart Show
8	The Waltons	18	The Wonderful World of Disney
9	Maude	=	The Rookies
10	Hawaii Five-O	20	Mannix
		=	Cannon

* Neilson Media Research 1974-'75 season of top-rated primetime television series in the USA.

Sitcoms remained popular, commanding seven of the top ten highest-ranking programs for 1974. In addition, a new wave of intense TV dramas was keeping us glued to our television sets. A slew of police, detective, or medical themed primetime TV programs hit our screens in the early '70s, and we were hooked. Medical or crime programs took eight of the top twenty placements.

The Mary Tyler Moore Show focused on the daily life of Mary Richards (played by Moore)—a financially independent working woman, which was still a rarity in the '70s. The show would win 29 Emmy Awards during its eight-year run, and launch three spin-offs: *Rhoda*, *Phyllis*, and *Lou Grant*.

Valerie Harper, Edward Asner, Cloris Leachman, Gavin MacLeod, Mary Tyler Moore, and Ted Knight in *The Mary Tyler Moore Show* (CBS. 1970–1977).

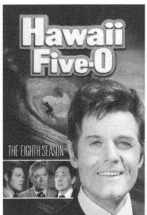

Zulu, Jack Lord, James MacArthur and Kam Fong in *Hawaii Five-O* (CBS. 1968-1980).

Airing for an impressive 12 seasons, *Hawaii Five-O* was largely shot on location in Honolulu. It followed a special police task force fighting organized crime across the Hawaiian Islands.

The original series ended in 1980, making it the longest running TV crime show at that time. A 2010 remake ran for ten seasons.

Melissa Sue Anderson, Karen Grassle, Michael Landon, Lindsay or Sidney Greenbush, and Melissa Gilbert, in *Little House on the Prairie* (NBC. 1974-1983).

Henry Winkler, Tom Bosley, Anson Williams, Marion Ross, Don Most, Erin Moran and Ron Howard in *Happy Days* (ABC. 1974-1984).

The television networks were quick to turn out new programs to keep us tuning in. Here are a few of the new programs that aired for the first time in '74: *Little House on the Prairie, Barney Miller, Happy Days, The Rockford Files, Derrick, Rhoda, Police Woman* and *Good Times*.

James Garner in *The Rockford Files* (NBC. 1974-1980).

Harold Gould, Nancy Walker, David Groh, Valerie Harper, and Julie Kavner, in *Rhoda* (CBS. 1974-1978).

Give the gift that makes TV more than something they just sit and watch: Odyssey.

Odyssey by Magnavox transforms any TV* into a challenging electronic playground of 12 fun-and-learning games the whole family can play and enjoy together.

Action and reaction games, like *Hockey* and *Tennis*. Arithmetic games, like *Analogic*. Geography games, like *States*. And pure fun games, like *Simon Says* and *Haunted House*.

So this year, give your family and friends the gift that makes TV more than something they just sit and watch. Give Odyssey.

Special Free Offer!
If you buy Odyssey before December 24, 1974, you get six extra games free: *Baseball, Handball, Volleyball, Wipe Out, Invasion* and *Fun Zoo*. Each a $5.95† value...all *free* with Odyssey now, at your Magnavox dealer.

ODYSSEY.
Electronic TV games from Magnavox.

Odyssey by Magnavox transforms any TV into a challenging electronic playground of 12 fun-and-learning games the whole family can play and enjoy together.

Action and reaction games, like *Hockey* and *Tennis*. Arithmetic games, like *Analogic*. Geography games, like *States*. And pure fun games, like *Simon Says* and *Haunted House*.

So this year, give your family and friends the gift that makes TV more than something they just sit and watch. Give Odyssey.

Odyssey. Electronic TV games from Magnavox.

Special Free Offer! If you buy Odyssey before December 24, 1974, you get six extra games free: *Baseball, Handball, Volleyball, Wipe Out, Invasion* and *Fun Zoo*. Each a $5.95 value...all *free* with Odyssey now, at your Magnavox dealer.

1974 in Cinema and Film

As cinema-goers, our interests and focus had shifted away from traditional classic Hollywood standards, which were often bounding with optimism and happy endings. We were seeking movies that offered more depth, more pain and a sense of reality.

Steve McQueen became the world's highest paid actor when he secured one million dollars plus a percentage of gross earnings for his role as chief fireman in *The Towering Inferno*.

Al Pacino and Robert De Niro star as Michael and young Vito Corleone in Francis Ford Coppola's *The Godfather Part II*.

By 1974, a new breed of directors including Francis Ford Coppola, Martin Scorsese, Stanly Kubrik and George Lucas, demanded more artistic control. They bravely tackled darker, more gritty, pessimistic themes of war, crime, depression and inner turmoil. The era of cinema houses owning their actors and controlling their directors had ended.

1974 film debuts

Tony Burton	The Black Godfather
Chevy Chase	The Groove Tube
Jeff Goldblum	Death Wish
Edward James Olmos	Black Fist
Kenneth Welsh	Piaf
Henry Winkler	Crazy Joe

* From en.wikipedia.org/wiki/1974_in_film.

American actor Jeff Goldblum has starred in some of the highest-grossing films of all time, including *Jurassic Park* (Universal, 1993), *Independance Day* (20th Century Fox, 1996), and *Guardians of the Galaxy* (Disney, 2017).

Top Grossing Films of the Year

1	The Towering Inferno	20th Century/Warner Bros.	$50,000,000
2	Blazing Saddles	Warner Bros. Pictures	$45,200,000
3	Young Frankenstein	20th Century Fox	$38,800,000
4	Earthquake	Universal Pictures	$36,300,000
5	The Trial of Billy Jack	Warner Bros. Pictures	$31,100,000
6	The Godfather Part II	Paramount Pictures	$30,700,000
7	Airport 1975	Universal Pictures	$25,800,000
8	The Longest Yard	Paramount Pictures	$23,000,000
9	The Life & Times of Grizzly Adams	Sunn Classic	$21,895,000
10	Murder on the Orient Express	Paramount Pictures	$19,124,000

* From en.wikipedia.org/wiki/1974_in_film by box office gross in the USA.

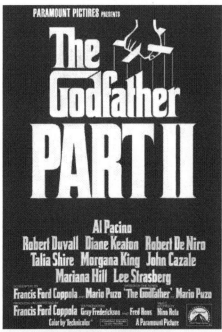

Francis Ford Coppola's *The Godfather Part II* won six Oscars (including Best Picture and Best Director) from eleven *Academy Award* nominations. It is ranked among the American Film Institute's greatest films of all time.

The Godfather Part II, The Trial of Billy Jack, and *Airport 1975* were all sequels to successful films of the early '70s.

The Trial of Billy Jack
Starring DELORES TAYLOR and TOM LAUGHLIN

A Decade of Disasters

The Poseidon Adventure
(20th Century Fox, 1972).

The Towering Inferno
(20th Century Fox, 1974).

The decade of the '70s saw the disaster movie genre reign supreme at the box office. Large casts, multiple plot lines, life or death calamities and impossible tales of survival kept us on the edge of our seats.

Earthquake (Universal, 1974).

Tidalwave (Toho, 1973).

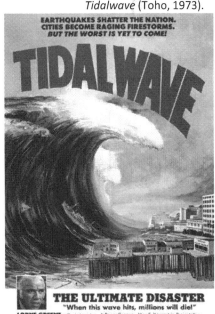

A- Big Ben Solid State. Here's the Big Ben that picks up the beat. The clock that knows what time it is stylewise, too. Brand new, inside and out. Solid-state electronic movement. Digital readout. Light-emitting diodes for soft illumination of digits. Up front controls...where you can find them, even on a sleepy morning. Two-tone styling in a clean, low-profile design. $49.95.

B- Big Ben. Classic keywound dependability. Luminous dial. $11.49.

C- Big Ben Sweep. Traditional styling. Luminous dial. Sweep second hand. Keywound. $13.95.

D- Big Ben Futura Deluxe. Sculptured case. Luminous dial. Keywound. $12.49.

Musical Memories

The early '70s saw musicians turn away from the joyful, chart-topping feel-good melodies of previous years, to pen expressively thoughtful lyrics dealing with the depths of our emotions and insecurities. This set the stage for the release of multiple seminal rock albums in the year 1973, where singer-songwriters like Carly Simon, Cat Stevens, James Taylor, Bruce Springsteen, Marvin Gaye, and Elton John, looked inwards, exploring their conflicts and anxieties, while Alice Cooper, Pink Floyd, Kiss, Led Zeppelin, Black Sabbath, Deep Purple, and others, reached out to the aimless and confused. It was arguably the greatest year in rock history.

What followed was 1974, a year music historians and critics find difficult to pin down. A wide mix of genres competed for dominance. Easy listening, pop, hard rock, heavy metal, country and soul music all gained #1 weekly placings. It must be noted that very few #1 songs on the Billboard Hot 100 stayed in that position for more than one week—an indication of the weakness of the year's singles to make any real impact.

Elton John's Greatest Hits album cover, 1974.

Olivier Newton John sings for UK in the *Eurovision Song Contest*, 1974.

The year's best selling album, *Elton John's Greatest Hits*, outsold the second place album, *Santana's Greatest Hits* by more than double. Both of these were compilation albums without any new songs.

John Denver gained his first (of four) #1 singles with *Sunshine On My Shoulders*, from the album of the same name. Meanwhile, Olivier Newton John secured her first (of five) #1 singles with *I Honestly Love You.*

During this period (1974 to 1977), disco reached its peak. From the counterculture dance clubs of the early '70s, disco emerged as an escape from the political and economic depressions of the era. Radio stations began playing non-stop disco segments, while record shops sold Disco Party LP mixes.

The Bee Gees and Donna Summer ruled as Kings and Queen of disco. While we were grooving to *Kung Fu Fighting* (Carl Douglas), and *Lady Marmalade* (Labelle), Motown joined in the disco fever–Diana Ross, Gladys Knight & the Pips, and the Jackson 5 were some of the Motown acts taking up disco rhythms.

The up-tempo heavy beats, energetic dance moves and glitzy fashions in the nightclubs, where race and sexual orientation became irrelevant, saw many disco songs top the charts. Club DJs began making a name for their "art" by mixing existing tracks and adding in reverb and other effects. Club drugs such as "poppers", "speed" and Quaaludes were dance floor favorites.

Above: The Bee Gees and Donna Summer.

Below: Abba, 1974.

6th April– Swedish band Abba won the *Eurovision Song Contest* held in Brighton, UK. Their winning song *Waterloo*, would become an international sensation. The song launched a string of hits for the band, putting them among the best-selling music artists of all time. In 2005, *Waterloo* was voted the best winning song in the competition's 50-year history.

1974 Billboard Top 30 Songs

	Artist	Song Title
1	Barbra Streisand	The Way We Were
2	Terry Jacks	Seasons In The Sun
3	Love Unlimited Orchestra	Love's Theme
4	Redbone	Come And Get Your Love
5	Jackson 5	Dancing Machine
6	Grand Funk Railroad	The Loco-Motion
7	MFSB	TSOP
8	Ray Stevens	The Streak
9	Elton John	Bennie And The Jets
10	Mac Davis	One Hell Of A Woman

Barbra Streisand, 1965.

Jackson 5, 1978.

Elton John on the Cher Show, 1975.

Aretha Franklin.

	Artist	Song Title
11	Aretha Franklin	Until You Come Back To Me
12	Kool and The Gang	Jungle Boogie
13	Maria Muldaur	Midnight At The Oasis
14	Stylistics	You Make Me Feel Brand New
15	Al Wilson	Show And Tell
16	Jim Stafford	Spiders And Snakes
17	David Essex	Rock On
18	John Denver	Sunshine On My Shoulder
19	Blue Magic	Sideshow
20	Blue Swede	Hooked On A Feeling

John Denver, 1975.   Paul McCartney, 1974.

	Artist	Song Title
21	Bo Donaldson and The Heywoods	Billy Don't Be A Hero
22	Paul McCartney and Wings	Band On The Run
23	Charlie Rich	The Most Beautiful Girl
24	Jim Croce	Time In A Bottle
25	John Denver	Annie's Song
26	Olivia Newton-John	Let Me Be There
27	Gordon Lightfoot	Sundown
28	Paul Anka	(You're) Having My Baby
29	Andy Kim	Rock Me Gently
30	Eddie Kendricks	Boogie Down

* From the *Billboard* top 30 singles of 1974.

There's not a wasted inch of space. Top, sides and front. Switches, toggle switches and dials.

Sony technology has mastered the portable radio.

Here's a list of things this radio can do.

First, and most important, it makes a tremendous sound. Only 8" high, the speaker is an oversized $4^3/_4$".

That's backed up by a powerful 2.8-watt (max.) output.

And that's backed up by a "Squelch Switch" to suppress interfering noise.

So what you end up with are the rich velvety tones that normally come out of radios too big to carry around.

There are three bands, FM, AM, and Public Service (Police car transmissions, for instance.)

A "moving film" style tuning dial.

And a 60-minute timer that turns the radio on and off.

Why not stop in at a Sony dealer and get checked out.

Then find a lonely stretch of road, and open her up.

The Cockpit. "It's a Sony."

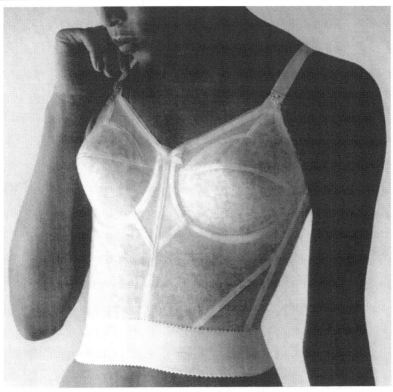

The Sears Ah-h Bra will go to any length to improve your shape.

The Sears Ah-h Bra will go to any length to improve your shape.

Our lace Ah-h Bra gives you a great shape. And now our new longline continues the good work all the way down to your waist.

But let's start at the top. Our wire is flat, so it lies flat to your body. In a soft channel of double-layered fabric, so it won't poke through. The top of the cup is elasticized to adapt to your fullness. The side boning is thin and flexible.

And our strap is unique. The stretch part is woven onto the nonstretch in one smooth piece. So you get just enough release to raise your arm without raising your entire bra.

It also has a 2" elastic band that won't roll up in front of pull up in the back.

Next to you is our Wonder-Fil lining. And the Perma-Prest fabric keeps its shape through many washings.

You'll find saleswomen in Sears Figure Shop who are trained to measure and fit you correctly. So come try on. And find out why we say "Ah-h."

At most Sears, Roebuck and Co. larger stores, through the catalog or call Catalog Shopping Service.

Sears. The Figure Shop.

Fashion Trends of the 1970s

By the early '70s, the fashion industry had lost its way, with designers and consumers alike seeking new directions and answers to the changing times. This was a decade without guidance and without rules. Trends caught on and shifted quickly. Fashions were varied and experimental. Pants got wider, skirts got shorter, and boots got taller. And within a season the trends reversed. Anything was possible, everything was acceptable.

Walking down any street you would have found skirts worn mini, midi, or full length. Pants could be slim-fit, wide, or bell-bottomed, hip-hugging or waist-clinching. Tops might be tie-dye swirl-patterned or bold solids. Shirts came long and loose, or tight and tailored.

Daywear pants-suit and skirt-suit.

Dresses came in all shapes and lengths too. They could be short Mod shifts, or calico lace prairie-style. They could be tailored with shirt-style collars and buttoned-down fronts. They could be long and loose caftans, flowing maxi-dresses, or waisted tailored-cut with belts and A-line skirts taken straight from the '50s.

Patchwork maxi-dresses by Yves Saint Laurent.

The hippie and psychedelic fashions of the late '60s were adopted and modified by mainstream non-hippies into more elegant structured forms. Caftans, prairie dresses, patchwork fabrics, shawls, tassels and beads hit the runways, and the streets, in the early '70s.

Elizabeth Taylor during her bohemian period, 1969.

Maudie James models Thea Porter patchwork dress, 1970.

Weipert and Burda fashion show, 1972.

In contrast to the hippie trends, Mod dresses of the early '60s made a comeback. Space-age synthetics and plastics, widely used in the '60s, were replaced with comfortable cottons and stretch knits. In winter, tunic dresses could be worn over turtlenecks, with woolen stockings or thigh-high boots.

Mod mini dresses worn with white boots or shoes, early 1970s.

The '70s were the first full decade where pants for women gained mainstream acceptance, and we couldn't get enough of them. Pants could be worn for any occasion—pants-suits for the office, silky patterns for evenings, or blocks and geometrics dressed down for daywear. And let's not forget blue jeans, the staple of casual wear for both men and women.

Day wear pants from the Sears Spring/ Summer catalog, 1970.

In the early '70s men and women wore their pants gently flared at the base. As the decade progressed, the flares got wider and wider, exploding into bell-bottoms by the mid-'70s.

Embroidered denim.

Flared knit polyester pants.

Flared silky jumpsuits.

Acme's got America wearing denims on their feet.

When Acme first introduced denim in our Acme Western boots and Dingo boots, it started a stampede. Since then, a lot of denim-come-latelys have stepped upon the scene. But still nobody makes denim boots like Acme.

We're the world's largest bootmaker, so you can be sure our denim boots are everything a denim boot should be.

And they're priced to leave you with some cash in your jeans.

When you're looking for denim boots, insist upon denims branded with Acme or Dingo.

Acme. Dingo. More boot for less bucks.

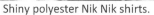
Shiny polyester Nik Nik shirts.   Stretch polyester.   Terry toweling jumpsuits.

Caught between the hippie and mod fashion extremes of the early '70s, the rest of us settled for easy-care. Whether it was casual, formal or business attire, being easy to wash and drip-dry dictated what we wore. Non-iron wool jersey knits and non-iron polyester were the material of choice for men and women throughout the '70s.

The '70s are often considered to be the decade that fashion forgot (or the decade of fashion that we would rather forget). And it's not hard to see why. Anything and everything became acceptable, no matter how outlandish or mismatched.

Here are some of our more questionable fashion decisions from the decade.

Shiny stretch
polyester jumpsuits.   Denim on denim.   Stretch knit pantsuits.   Safari suits.

John Travolta in *Saturday Night Fever*
(Paramount Pictures, 1977).

Dancer at Studio 54, New York.

And then there was disco.
It shone so brightly. It glittered so briefly.
And in a flash, it was gone.

Model wears
sequined jumpsuit.

Sporting silver
lamé jumpsuits.

Dancers at Studio 54, New York.

Menswear from the *Sears* Home Shopping Catalog, Winter 1974.

Also in Sports

24th Jan-2nd Feb– The 1974 British Commonwealth Games was held in Christchurch, New Zealand. More than 1,200 athletes from 38 nations took part. The Games' TV coverage marked the introduction of color TV broadcasts in New Zealand.

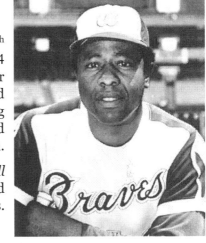

8th Apr– Hank Aaron hit his 715th home run, beating Babe Ruth's 714 home run record set in 1935. For several months prior, Aaron had received tons of hate mail, including death threats, from people who did not want Babe Ruth's record broken.

Aaron was inducted into the *Baseball Hall of Fame* in 1982, having finished his career with 755 home runs.

15th-16th June– Chris Evert and Bjorn Born won their first Grand Slam titles at the French Open. Evert would go on to win 18 Grand Slam singles titles, reigning as the #1 singles tennis player over 7 years. Borg would go on to win 11 Grand Slam singles titles, including five consecutive Wimbledon wins.

7th July– West Germany won the 1974 FIFA World Cup in Munich. On 22nd June, East and West German teams played against each other for the first and only time during the countries' 41-year separation.

30th Oct– "The Rumble in the Jungle" took place in Kinshasa, Zaire. Muhammad Ali regained the Heavyweight title knocking out George Foreman in 8 rounds. The title had been stripped from Ali in 1967 following his anti-war stance and Army draft refusal.

The ball Hank and The Babe hit.

Since Major League Baseball began, one ball has been in every play of every inning of every game. Spalding.

The same Spalding quality goes into every baseball product we make: balls, gloves, bats and protective equipment for Little League on up through the Majors.

Baseball is how we got started. We're glad to be a part of it.

Way to go, Hank.

Way to go, Babe.

Spalding. The name the game grew up with.

Other News from 1974

3rd Mar– Turkish Airlines Flight 981 crashed near Paris killing all 346 passengers and crew aboard. The plane was en route to London.

8th Mar– Charles de Gaulle Airport opened in Paris, France. The circular avant-garde building was designed by Architect Paul Andreu.

2nd Apr– French President Georges Pompidou died while in Office to the surprise of the nation. His terminal illness, a rare blood cancer, had been concealed from the public. He was 63 years old.

3rd-4th Apr– A series of 127 tornadoes, the largest tornado family ever recorded, tore through 13 states in central USA and parts of Canada. More than 300 people were killed with many thousands injured and hundreds of millions of dollars in damage.

April 1974– Three Navajo men were beaten and killed by white teenagers in the town of Farmington, New Mexico. The perpetrators were sent to reform school for their crime. Protests highlighted the problem of discrimination and violence against Native Americans. Abuse, torture, and murder, known as "Indian Rolling", had become routine activities committed by white youth in the Farmington area.

11th May– A major earthquake of magnitude 7.1 struck China's Yunnan province causing up to 20,000 deaths.

29th Jun– Isabel Perón was sworn in as the first female President of Argentina, replacing her sick husband Juan Perón just two days before his death.

16th Jul– The Greece-backed Cypriot National Guard staged a coup d'état to remove President Makarios III of Cyprus and install Greek Cypriot Nikos Sampson as acting President. Makarios fled to London. He reported to the UN that Cyprus had been invaded by Greece.

20th Jul– Turkey sent troops to invade Cyprus, capturing 36% of the land, and creating a divide known as the Green Line. Following a ceasefire in August, 200,000 Cypriots resettled–Greek Cypriots moved south of the Green Line while Turkish Cypriots moved north.

4th Aug– Italian neo-fascists detonated a bomb on a train between Italy and West Germany. Twelve people were killed with many more injured.

6th Aug– The Pan American World Airways lobby at Los Angeles International Airport was bombed, killing three.

7th Aug– French acrobat Philippe Petit walked across a high wire slung between the twin towers of the World Trade Center in New York. The unauthorized act took six years to plan, involving fake ID cards for access, and a bow and arrow for shooting a wire between towers. Petit performed for 45 minutes on the high wire before surrendering to police.

30th Aug– 153 passengers were killed when an express train traveling from Belgrade to Germany derailed in Zagreb. The investigation that followed showed the train had been travelling up to 43 m/h (70 km/h) faster than the speed limit, and that the brakes had been applied too late. The driver and assistant claimed they were at fault due to exhaustion caused by excessive hours worked prior to the accident.

8th Sep– A terrorist bomb exploded on TWA Flight 841 from Tel Aviv to New York City shortly after takeoff from a transit stop in Athens. The plane crashed into the Ionian Sea killing all aboard. The perpetrators were never identified.

12th Sep– Emperor Haile Selassie of Ethiopia was deposed by the country's armed forces. The Soviet-backed coup d'état brought an end to the reign of the House of Solomon, which had ruled since 1270. The coup was immediately followed by a bloody civil war, which continued until 1991.

1974– The Rubiks Cube was invented by Hungarian sculptor and professor of architecture Ernő Rubik. Designed as a teaching aid for his students, the cube quickly became the most popular puzzle toy in the world.

The original wooden "magic cube" prototype created by Ernő Rubik.

Famous People Born in 1974

12th Jan– Mel C (Melanie Jayne Chisholm), English singer (Spice Girls).

16th Jan– Kate Moss, English model.

30th Jan– Christian Bale, British actor.

30th Jan– Olivia Coleman, English actress.

10th Feb– Elizabeth Banks, American actress.

13h Feb– Robbie Williams, English singer.

16th Feb– Mahershala Ali, American actor.

22nd Feb– James Blunt, English musician.

5th Mar– Eva Mendes, American actress.

5th Mar– Matt Lucas, English comedian.

17th Apr– Victoria Beckham, English singer (The Spice Girls) & fashion designer.

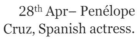

28th Apr– Penélope Cruz, Spanish actress.

30th May– Cee-Lo Green [Thomas Callaway], American record producer, singer-songwriter & actor.

1st Jun– Alanis Morissette, Canadian-American singer.

7th Jun– David Filoni, American director, producer, & screenwriter.

7th Jun– Edward "Bear" Grylls, British adventurer, author & TV presenter.

26th Jun– Derek Jeter, American Baseball HOF shortstop (14 × MLB All-Star).

10th Jul– Chiwetel Ejiofor, British film & stage actor.

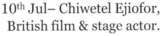

14th Jul– David Mitchell, English comedian & actor.

25th Jul– Paul Epworth, British record producer, musician, & songwriter.

30th Jul– Hilary Swank, American actress.

20th Aug– Amy Adams, American actress.

31st Aug– Andrei Medvedev, Ukrainian tennis player.

31st Aug– Marc Webb, American music video, TV, & film director

1st Sep– Jason Taylor, American Pro Football HOF linebacker.

10th Oct– Dale Earnhardt Jr., American auto racer, team owner & broadcaster.

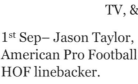

19th Sep– Jimmy Fallon, American actor & comedian.

11th Nov– Leonardo DiCaprio, American actor.

28th Oct– Joaquin Phoenix, American actor.

17th Dec– Sarah Paulson, American actress.

18th Nov– Chloë Sevigny, American actress.

24th Dec– Ryan Seacrest, American DJ & television host.

19th Dec– Ricky Ponting, Australian cricket batsman, captain, coach & broadcaster (168 Tests).

The Challenger. New Viceroy Extra Milds.

The one cigarette with lowered tar but lots of taste.
Compare the taste with other low tar cigarettes...it's really no contest.

Census Statistics [1]

- Population of the world   4.00 billion
- Population in the United States   209.28 million
- Population in the United Kingdom   56.09 million
- Population in Canada   22.75 million
- Population in Australia   13.61 million
- Average age for marriage of women   21.1 years old
- Average age for marriage of men   23.1 years old
- Average family income USA $12,840 / year
- Unemployment rate USA   7.2 %

Costs of Goods [2]

- Average new house $29,966
- Average new car $4,095
- A gallon of gasoline $0.39
- Bread $0.41 per 2 pound
- Coffee, Maxwell House $1.89 per 2 pound
- Peanut Butter, Skippy $0.55 per 12 oz jar
- Oranges, Florida $0.59 for 10
- Pineapples, fresh whole $1.00 for 3
- Mayonnaise, Kraft $0.89 per quart jar
- Soda, Pepsi Cola 12 oz cans $0.88 per 6 cans
- Fresh eggs $0.58 per dozen
- Ketchup, Heinz $0.25 per 14 oz bottle
- Laundry soap, Fab $0.32 per 20 oz box
- Cinema ticket $1.00

[1] Figures taken from worldometers.info/world-population, US National Center for Health Statistics, *Divorce and Divorce Rates* US (cdc.gov/nchs/data/series/sr_21/sr21_029.pdf) and United States Census Bureau, *Historical Marital Status Tables* (census.gov/data/tables/time-series/demo/families/marital.html).
[2] Figures from thepeoplehistory.com, mclib.info/reference/local-history & dqydj.com/historical-home-prices/.

Let's get it together.

These words first appeared in print in the year 1974.

probiotic

nanotechnology

shuttle diplomacy

biofeul

telecommute

SUPERMOM

Junk bond

Smoking gun

ditzy

bunker mentality

Touch screen

CT scan

Afro-Latino

transgender

memory card

wake-up call

GOTCHA

* From merriam-webster.com/time-traveler/1974.

A heartfelt plea from the author:

I sincerely hope you enjoyed reading this book and that it brought back many fond memories from the past.

Success as an author has become increasingly difficult with the proliferation of **AI generated** copycat books by unscrupulous sellers. They are clever enough to escape copyright action and use dark web tactics to secure paid-for **fake reviews**, something I would never do.

Hence I would like to ask you—I plead with you—the reader, to leave a star rating or review on Amazon. This helps make my book discoverable for new readers, and helps me to compete fairly against the devious copycats.

If this book was a gift to you, you can leave stars or a review on your own Amazon account, or you can ask the gift-giver or a family member to do this on your behalf.

I have enjoyed researching and writing this book for you and would greatly appreciate your feedback.

Best regards,
Bernard Bradforsand-Tyler.

Please leave a
book review/rating at:

https://bit.ly/1974reviews

Or scan the QR code:

Flashback books make the perfect gift-
see the full range at

https://bit.ly/FlashbackSeries

Image Attributions

Photographs and images used in this book are reproduced courtesy of:

Page 6 – From *Hot Rod* magazine, Jul 1974 (PD image).*
Page 8 – Impeach Nixon protestors in 1974. Creator unknown. Pre-1978, no copyright mark (PD image).
Page 9 – Palm Beach International Concert, May 1974. Pre-1978, no copyright mark (PD image).
Page 10 – 1974 print magazine advertisement for the US Army (PD image).*
Page 11 – College girls 1973 by Ed Uthman. Source: en.wikipedia.org/wiki/Youth#/media/File:
1970sgirls.jpg. Attribution CC BY-SA 2.0. – NOW conference in Houston, May 1974.
Source:radcliffe.harvard.edu/schlesinger-library/collections/records-of-the-national-organization-for-
women. Photos this page are pre-1978, no copyright mark (PD image).
Page 12 – From *Readers Digest* magazine, Dec 1974 (PD image).*
Page 13 – 1974 print magazine advertisement for Polaroid (PD image).*
Page 14 – Tyneside street protest in 1974, unknown creator, from the ChronicleLive archive.
Source: chroniclelive.co.uk/news/history/gallery/tyneside-1974-new-byker-wall-21734884. Pre-1978,
no copyright mark (PD image).
Page 15 – Women's march in London, from the Times Photographic Archive, March 1974.
– Boy crossing road, date and creator unknown. Images this page are pre-1978. Where images are not
in the public domain, they are included here for information only under US fair use laws due to: 1-
images are low resolution copies; 2- images do not devalue the ability of the copyright holders to profit
from the original works in any way; 3- Images are too small to be used to make illegal copies for use in
another book; 4- The images are relevant to the article created.
Page 16 – 1974 print magazine advertisement for Kodak (PD image).*
Page 17 – London teachers' march, 1974, creator unknown. Source: bishopsgate.org.uk/stories/gallery-
the-gay-liberation-front-the-origins-of-pride. Pre-1978, no copyright mark (PD image). – Nurses' strike,
1974, creator unknown, from the Shropshire Star. Pre-1978, no copyright mark (PD image).
Page 18 – From *Popular Science* magazine, Apr 1974 (PD image).*
Page 19 – From *Ebony* magazine, May 1974 (PD image).*
Page 20 – Commune members, source: allthatsinteresting.com/hippie-communes.
– Commune members pose in front of a tipi, by John Olson from Life Magazine, 18th Jul 1969. Source:
books.google.com/books?id =K08EAAAAMBAJ&printsec. Pre-1978, no copyright mark (PD image).
Page 21 – Tending to the fields, source: burlingtonfreepress.com/story/news/local/vermont/
2015/07/24/vermont-remains-hippie-epicenter/30564907/, photo by Rebecca Lepkoff of Vermont
Historical Society. – Geodesic dome, source: vpr.org/post/communes-hippie-invasion-and-how-1970s-
changed-state#stream/0 by Kate Daloz. – Commune bus, source: allthatsinteresting.com/hippie-
communes. All images this page are pre-1978, no copyright mark (PD images).
Page 22 – 1974 print magazine advertisement for Ford (PD image).*
Page 23 – Friday afternoon traffic heading out of Atlanta, by Al Stephenson / AJC file. Source:
ajc.com/lifestyles/flashback-photos-through-the-years-1951-1997/ByK7dbup2R66nM4TMIWX9O/.
– Waiting for gas, creator unknown, 1974.
Page 24 – Images taken from 1974 print magazine advertisements for Ford Mustang II, Chrysler
Plymouth Gold Duster, and Mercury Comet GT (PD images).*
Page 25 – Images taken from 1974 print magazine advertisements for Datsun 710, Porsche 2.0, and
Volks Wagen Beetle (PD images).*
Page 26 – 1974 print magazine advertisement for Ford (PD image).*
Page 27 – From *Ebony* magazine, Feb 1974 (PD image).*
Page 28 – 1974 headlines and movie posters by Warner Bros. and 20th Century Fox. (PD images).**
Page 29 – Demonstrators outside the White House, by Marion S. Trikosko or Thomas J. O'Halloran.
– Leaving the White House, the White House Photo Office Collection (Nixon Admin) catalog.archives.
gov/id/66394380' – Gerald Ford, by David Hume Kennerly - U.S. National Archives and Records Admin.
All photos this page are the work of a US Government employee and are in the Public Domain.
Page 30 – Egyptian forces cross the Suez Canal, from *Military Battles on the Egyptian Front* by Gammal
Hammad. Published by Dār al-Shurūq, Egypt. Source: en.wikipedia.org/wiki/Operation_Badr_(1973)
(PD image). – Israeli soldiers by the Israel Defense Forces. Source: commons.wikimedia.org/wiki/
Category:Yom_Kippur_War (PD image).
Page 31 – Speed limit and No Gas station, creators unknown. Source: commons.wikimedia.org/wiki/
Category: Gas_ shortage_of_1973_in_the_United_States. Images this page pre-1978, no copyright
mark (PD images).
Page 32 – 1974 print magazine advertisement for Yamaha (PD image).*
Page 33 – Images from Boston busings protests of 1974. Creators unknown. Images this page are pre-
1978. Where images are not in the public domain, they are included here for information only under
US fair use laws due to: 1- images are low resolution copies; 2- images do not devalue the ability of the
copyright holders to profit from the original works in any way; 3- Images are too small to be used to
make illegal copies for use in another book; 4- The images are relevant to the article created.
Page 34 – 1974 print magazine advertisement for Bell Telephone Company (PD image).*
Page 35 – *Operation Emery Baneberry* at Nevada Proving Grounds, 18th Dec 1970. – *Operation Smiling
Buddha,* Rajasthan, 18th May 1974. Photos this page by US Army and are in the public domain.

Page 36 – Mainland Campaign, London and Birmingham 1974, creator unknown. Images this page are pre-1978. Where images are not in the public domain, they are included here for information only under US fair use laws due to: 1- images are low resolution copies; 2- images do not devalue the ability of the copyright holders to profit from the original works in any way; 3- Images are too small to be used to make illegal copies for use in another book; 4- The images are relevant to the article created.

Page 37 – Creators unknown. Images this page are pre-1978. Where images are not in the public domain, they are included here for information only under US fair use laws due to: 1- images are low resolution copies; 2- images do not devalue the ability of the copyright holders to profit from the original works in any way; 3- Images are too small to be used to make illegal copies for use in another book; 4- The images are relevant to the article created.

Page 38 – Portuguese soldiers and street celebrations, creators unknown, 25th Apr 1974. Source: en.wikipedia.org/wiki/ Carnation_Revolutio. Attribution: CC BY 4.0. – Street march in 1973, creator unknown. Source: nzhistory.govt.nz/media/photo/pro-abortion-march-1973 (PD image).*

Page 39 – Creators unknown. Images this page are pre-1978. Where images are not in the public domain, they are included here for information only under US fair use laws due to: 1- images are low resolution copies; 2- images do not devalue the ability of the copyright holders to profit from the original works in any way; 3- Images are too small to be used to make illegal copies for use in another book; 4- The images are relevant to the article created.

Page 40 – 1974 print magazine advertisement for Delta (PD image).*

Page 41 – From *Motor Trend* magazine, Apr 1974 (PD image).*

Page 42 – Nixon signs ESA, creator unknown, 28th Dec 1973. Source: politico.com/story/2012/12/this-day-in-politics-085535. – Eagle and Gray wolf from USFWS Endangered Species, creators unknown. Sources: en.wikipedia.org/wiki/ Bald_eagle#/media/File:About_to_Launch_(26075320352).jpg and commons.wikimedia.org/wiki/File:Endangered_gray_wolf_%28Canis_lupus%29.jpg (PD images).*

Page 43 – Terracotta army, photos by Dennis Jarvis and Windmemories. Source: commons.wikimedia. org/wiki/Category:Terracotta_Army. Creative commons attribution share alike CC BY-SA 4.0.

Page 44 – 1974 print magazine advertisement for Magnavox (PD image).*

Page 45 – *All in the Family* screen still, 4th May 1971, by CBS Television.** Source: en.wikipedia.org/wiki/All_in_the_Family #/media/File: Archie_and_Lionel_All_in_the_Family_1971.JPG.

Page 46 – *The Mary Tyler Moore Show* publicity image by CBS, 1970.** Source: commons.wikimedia. org/wiki/Mary_ Tyler_Moore_cast_1970_1977.JPG. (PD image). – Still image and poster from the TV series *Hawaii Five-0* by CBS, 1970.**

Page 47 – Publicity photo for *Little House on the Prairie* by NBC, 1974.** – Publicity photo for *Happy Days* by ABC, 1974.** – Screen Still of James Garner in *The Rockford Files,* NBC. 1974.** – Publicity photo for *Rhoda* by CBS, 1974.**

Page 48 – From *Readers Digest* Magazine Dec 1974. Source: ebay.com (PD image).*

Page 49 – Publicity still for Steve McQueen taken in 1966. – Al Pacino and Robert De Niro on the set of The Godfathers Part 2. – Jeff Goldblum in 2017. Source: commons.wikimedia.org/wiki/Category: Jeff_Goldblum_in_2017 (PD image).* Images this page, where not in the public domain, are included here for information only under US fair use laws due to: 1- images are low resolution copies; 2- images do not devalue the ability of the copyright holders to profit from the original works in any way; 3- Images are too small to be used to make illegal copies for use in another book; 4- The images are relevant to the article created.

Page 50 – Film posters for the movies *The Godfather Part II* by Paramount Pictures, 1974.** – *Airport 1975* by Universal Pictures, 1974.** – *The Trial of Billy Jack* by Warner Bros. Pictures, 1974.**

Page 51 – Film posters for the movies *The Poseidon Adventure* by 20th Century Fox, 1972.** – *The Towering Inferno* by 20th Century Fox, Warner Bros, 1974.** – *Earthquake* by Universal Pictures, 1974.** – *Tidal Wave* by Toho Company, 1973.**

Page 52 – 1974 print magazine advertisement for Westclox (PD image).*

Page 53 – 1974 print magazine advertisement for Panasonic (PD image).*

Page 54 – Elton John's Greatest Hits album cover by MCA/Polydor, 1974. – Olivier Newton John screen capture from the *Eurovision Song Contest*, 1974. These images are included here for information only under US fair use laws due to: 1- images are low resolution copies; 2- images do not devalue the ability of the copyright holders to profit from the original works in any way; 3- Images are too small to be used to make illegal copies for use in another book; 4- The images are relevant to the article created.

Page 55 – The Bee Gees on *The Midnight Special*, NBC TV, 1973 Source: commons.wikimedia.org/wiki/ Category:Bee_ Gees. – Donna Summer publicity photo by Francesco Scavullo for Casablanca Records. Source: commons.wikimedia.org/wiki/Category:Donna_Summer_in_1974. – Abba publicity photo for AVRO's *TopPop*, Holland TV. Source: commons.wikimedia.org/wiki/Category:Members_of_ABBA. Photos this page are pre-1978, no copyright marks (PD images).

Page 56 – Barbra Streisand from *My Name is Barbra* CBS TV special, 1965. Source: commons.wikimedia. org/wiki/Category:Barbra_Streisand. – Jackson 5 publicity photo. Source: commons.wikimedia.org/ wiki/Category:The_Jackson_5. – Elton John from *The Cher Show*, CBS Television. Source: commons.wikimedia.org/wiki/Category:Elton_John_in_1975. – Aretha Franklin from Billboard, 17 February 1968. Source: commons. wikimedia.org/wiki/Category:Cher_(singer)_in_1973. All photos this page are pre-1978, no copyright marks (PD images).

Page 57 – John Denver publicity photo for RCA records, 9th Aug 1973. Source: commons.wikimedia. org/wiki/Category: John_Denver. Pre-1978, no copyright mark (PD image). – Paul McCartney performing with Wings, 5th Aug 1972 in Finland. Source: commons.wikimedia.org/wiki/Category:Paul_ McCartney. Photos this page are pre-1978, no mark (PD images).
Page 58 – 1974 print magazine advertisement for Sony (PD image).*
Page 59 – From Ebony magazine, Feb 1974 (PD image).*
Page 60 – Pants and skirt-suit, 1969, creator unknown. Pre-1978, (PD image).– Maxi-dress by YSL, Spring-Summer 1969. Source: minniemuse.com/articles/creative-connections/ patchwork. (PD image).
Page 61 – Elizabeth Taylor, source: instyle.com/celebrity/transformations/elizabeth-taylors-changing-looks. – Thea Porter dress, photographer Patrick Hunt, 1970. – Weipert and Burda fashion show, Apr 1972, photo by Friedrich Magnussen. Permission CC BY-SA 3.0 DE. – Mini dresses, sources: pinterest.com/pin/99782947967669796/ and retrospace.org/2011_01_01_archive.html unknown photographers. Pre-1978, no copyright mark (PD image).
Page 62 – Fashions from Sears Catalogues, Pre-1978, no copyright mark (PD image). – Hungarian singer Szűcs Judit wears embroidered demin. Source: commons.wikimedia.org/wiki/File:Szűcs_Judit_ énekesnő._Fortepan_88657.jpg. Licensed under the Creative Commons Attribution-Share Alike 3.0 Unported. – Knit polyester pants from the 1975 J.C. Penney catalog. Pre-1978, no copyright marks (PD image). – Flared jumpsuits, creator unknown. Pre-1978, no marks (PD images).
Page 63 – From Motor Trend magazine Nov 1974 (PD image).*
Page 64 – Nik Nik shirts, polyester jumpsuits, and knit pantsuits, source: onedio.com/haber/erkekte-retro-modasinin-tutmamasinin-32-mantikli-sebebi-300983. – Polyester tops and pants, toweling jumpsuits, and shrink tops by Colombia Minerva, source: flashbak.com/the-good-the-bad-and-the-tacky-20-fashion-trends-of-the-1970s-26213/. – Denim on denim source: typesofjeanfits.com/a-brief-history-of-jeans-denim-history-timeline/. – Safari suits source: klyker.com/ 1970s-fashion/. All images this page Pre-1978, no copyright mark or renewal (PD image).
Page 65 – Still image from Saturday Night Fever by Paramount Pictures.** Source: vocal.media/beat/ the-list-saturday-night-fever-40th-anniversary. – Dancers Studio 54, sources: definition.org/ studio-54/2/ & alexilubomirski.com/image-collections/studio-54. Pre-1978, no copyright marks (PD image).
Page 66 – From the Sears Home Shopping Catalog Winter 1974 (PD image).*
Page 67 – Hank Aaron in 1974, creator unknown. Source: commons.wikimedia.org/wiki/Category: Hank_ Aaron. Pre-1978 (PD image). – Ali KOs Forman, 30th Oct 1974, creator unknown. Source: commons.wikimedia.org/wiki/Category:Foreman_v_Ali,_30_October_1974 Pre-1978 (PD image).
Page 68 – 1974 print magazine advertisement for Spalding (PD image).*
Page 69-71– President Georges Pompidou in 1969. Source: commons.wikimedia.org/wiki/Category: Georges_Pompidou. – Navajo protest march, 1974, by Bob Fitch. – Isabel Peron by Movimiento Nacional Peronista. Source: en.wikipedia.org/wiki/File:Isabel_peron_ banda_presidencial_y_ bastón.png (PD image). – Turkish troops invade Cyprus, creator unknown.– Philippe Petit crosses between the Twin Towers, by Alan Welner/AP Photo. – Original wooden prototype for the Rubiks cube, by Erno Rubik. All photos these pages are pre-1978 and are likely to be in the public domain. Where not in the public domain, they are included here for information only under US fair use laws due to: 1- images are low resolution copies; 2- images do not devalue the ability of the copyright holders to profit from the original works in any way; 3- Images are too small to be used to make illegal copies for use in another book; 4- The images are relevant to the article created.
Pages 72-74– All photos are, where possible, CC BY 2.0 or PD images made available by the creator for free use including commercial use. Where commercial use photos are unavailable, photos are included here for information only under US fair use laws due to: 1- images are low resolution copies; 2- images do not devalue the ability of the copyright holders to profit from the original works in any way; 3- Images are too small to be used to make illegal copies for use in another book; 4- The images are relevant to the article created.
Page 75 – From Popular Mechanics magazine, May 1973 (PD image).*
Page 78 – 1974 print magazine advertisement for Imperial (PD image).*
Page 79 – From Ebony magazine, May 1974 (PD image).*

*Advertisement (or image from an advertisement) is in the public domain because it was published in a collective work (such as a periodical issue) in the US between 1925 and 1977 and without a copyright notice specific to the advertisement.
**Posters for movies or events are either in the public domain (published in the US between 1925 and 1977 and without a copyright notice specific to the artwork) or owned by the production company, creator, or distributor of the movie or event. Posters, where not in the public domain, and screen stills from movies or TV shows, are reproduced here under USA Fair Use laws due to: 1- images are low resolution copies; 2- images do not devalue the ability of the copyright holders to profit from the original works in any way; 3- Images are too small to be used to make illegal copies for use in another book; 4- The images are relevant to the article created.

First printed in 2023 in the USA (ISBN 978-1-922676-10-8).
Self-published by B. Bradforsand-Tyler.

Made in United States
Troutdale, OR
02/06/2024